Only Now

POEMS

Stuart Kestenbaum

To Jean —

[signature]

8/14

DEERBROOK EDITIONS

PUBLISHED BY
Deerbrook Editions
P.O. Box 542
Cumberland, ME 04021
207.829.5038
www.deerbrookeditions.com

FIRST EDITION
© 2014 by Stuart Kestenbaum
Page 75 constitutes an extension of this page.
All rights reserved.

ISBN: 978-0-9828100-9-5

Contents

For Susan

Prayer While Downshifting

Driving into town just past dusk I see the gas station sign
lit up and underneath the brand and the price in big
white letters *self-service* as if this is not just a place
to buy gas and get chips and beer, but the place where
you can take yourself in for your own repairs, making sure
to change the soul's oil frequently, checking the timing belt
with every 60,000 emotional miles, making sure the air filter
isn't clogged with the dirt of the dreamless road because
we've got to keep track of these things, for who else
will these days, and when we're done we can drive down
to the self-storage units at the edge of town, so many selves
in those metal-sided buildings. We can open the padlock
and rummage through the windowless room, discover
who we were, not just the golden highlights
but the total incarnation, pacing the concrete floors
or sitting on the couch that we don't need anymore
listening to our own stories, all the troubles we used to have.

Rocky Coast

First there was the pink granite
molten and buried for 350 million years,

then there was the ice encountering the ledge
dragging rocks and trees over the land

and then the lichen working in the cold, ceaseless wind,
cleaving to the stone, resurrecting the soil by eating away

at the mica and quartz to make a thin layer of earth
that the coast rests on. And then there was the Dunkin' Donuts

built on the ledge in 1989 in Bucksport, Maine, the town where
the paper mill makes clouds and sends them billowing

out into the landscape, the Dunkin' Donuts where
the coffee is always fresh and when you inhale its aroma

it's as if you are starting the day again or starting
your life over. One more chance. This is where I buy

my chocolate sugar donut and drive down Route 15 in the dark,
when I bite down on an earring-back baked into it.

I dream of the million-dollar liability settlement, enough
to do whatever I would want to, and return

to show with horror the small steel post to the young woman
in bright polyester at the counter who offers me a dozen

free donuts, not enough to change my life, but
enough to feed me for a while, and what else

could you need: sugar, fat, and the first bite,
like Eve's, just before she walked out into the fallen world.

Getting There

Where is the place we are always asking about.
It's the country we remember in our dreams.
Where is where we'll find what we need to know

whatever that is, whatever we thought it was
going to be. Suddenly the answer will be there
to which we will say, "Where on earth

did that come from?" and it will have come
from deep inside us, the place we didn't even know existed,
where all the answers are waiting patiently.

We are amazed that an answer so vibrant,
so without pretense, so right, could have existed
inside us, as if this is the job of some organ

within our bodies, to produce things we knew all along
but didn't recognize, like some quiet street or trail
where we are walking and someone is calling out our name,

where we stop to listen and can hear what was there all along:
the water dropping from leaf to leaf, the syncopation
of air and green and small birds that are hidden in the branches

singing the only song they know, over and over and over
and over into the twilight where the world merges
into one color, one shade, and one breath.

The Next World

We throw away so many things, pack them into translucent
garbage bags where you can see through to the once beloved objects.
The humbling moment is to realize it's all heading to the dumpster,
not just my journal and last month's bills, but all of history,
and all that will be left is an ember rotating in space.
Don't worry, it will all start over again. This isn't the only world,
this is just one try at it. This is the world that had ice and snow,
this is the world where the apple blossoms fell to earth,
this is the world where the clapboarded churches stood
so white against the blue sky, like a remarkable original idea
that gets our attention. When this world goes someone will build
another one and somewhere at the mom and pop store
next to the coffee and non-dairy creamer the angels
will be gathered around remembering this one
with nostalgia and a bit of sadness, the way we always remember
the thing that has passed, the fallen petals, the fallen leaves,
the door to the abandoned house partially unhinged and swinging
in the wind. In the next world the old letters and bills
will fall like snow, white upon white of special deals
and eternal promises of love. The next world will wait
for the sun to rise for the first time over the hills
we haven't named yet. All of the cars will still be asleep
and the traffic lights will wait expectantly like kids
on the first day of school, before you know all that order
doesn't make sense. The traffic lights will wait to turn,
wait for the honk of now and the day breaking.
We'll all get started again only this time
we'll get it right, this time we'll think with our
bodies and our hands, this time we won't write anything down,
we will just learn to listen, not only to each other,
but to the beat of birds' wings, not only to our
own inner whisper, but to everything that's
whispering around us. I'm quiet now. I'm ready for the next world,
ready for the ice to rumble across the pond, ready to glide
over the surface of this new place, where there's no trash

in the gutter yet, no love lost, no discouraging words
and every heart is open for business,
cash only, no checks or credit cards accepted.

Waking

If we didn't imagine our own lives every morning
then the next step wouldn't be possible,
and we wouldn't find ourselves brushing our teeth
or staring out the window.
We don't have to imagine all of the day, just the first
moment as if every morning we are once again
emerging from the birth canal
and entering into the room of our own being.
Here for another day. One day we'll stop imagining
that first moment, stop imagining the road outside,
the light snow falling, the newspaper being shoved
into its tube at the end of the driveway.
Then it will be all over and we will have
slipped somewhere else. What will we imagine then?
The shadows of trees, the hunger for another day?
Perhaps someone will imagine us, imagine we are possible
and we will rise again and start doing things in the world,
only no one else will hear us, like yesterday
during a conference call when I was trying to talk
but my mute button was on—the conversation is going on
without me, even though I think that I have
something to say. We always think we've got something to say,
something that can add to the dialogue, but maybe we don't.
Maybe there is no dialogue, only each of us imagining our lives
or each other's lives. Some mornings you don't imagine
yourself right away. It takes a few heartbeats
and a few breaths like an old car starting in winter,
the cranks and groans of the engine before ignition.
In that gap we can see everything. We can see the world
before we were in it, when it was all clouds and endless sky,
when it was shadows. It's the shadows that let you know
that there is something behind all this, the shadows
that describe the life of the solid objects that the light
can't pass through. We've awoken in a planet full of life.
We are breathing in this body, this collection of cells
so specialized as to make the world appear before our eyes again,
to have the blood circulate through our veins and arteries

like the rivers of a great undiscovered country,
the day just beginning, the day breaking as it always does,
whether we expect it to or not.

Winter Morning Prayer

When the day falls out of the sky
it is as surprised as I am to see
all this sunrise splashing at my feet,
to see the walls of the mountains described,
the tops of the spruce trees dipped
in snow as if they are ready to write down
their own story in this first light that is falling on
the yellow school buses and silver mail boxes
and the dark road and on my breath that I exhale
in the cold morning, how it drifts off
in small clouds of silence.

Crows

Yesterday I was reading about the difference between
will and *shall*, how these ancient words moved
from Old German to Old English and mutated into
different ways that we might see the world or not,
and I realized that I am not even fluent in my own tongue
let alone someone else's. The words themselves have traveled
great distances and changed their spellings but tried to keep
their hearts in the heart of what they say, beating inside
the new typography and pronunciations. It's always a wonder
to speak another tongue, to say *beer* in Mandarin
and have everyone at the table smile with just two syllables
that are probably only somewhat recognizable thanks
to the empty glass. And beyond human language everyone
is talking. The crows not only have a language but also
a dialect and I wonder if some of them have a passing
knowledge of raven, the way a promising student
writes on her resume that she knows conversational French.
And do the chickadees understand crow or is it just so many caws,
interference on the airwaves? Maybe all the animals complain
about the mixed signals they're getting, the barks and snorts
and yips and howls, the chirps and song. No one has translated
any of this yet, the poetry of the coyote or the hymns of gulls.
The air is full of language and somewhere along the way
we began to hear it and make it into our own sounds
and my sound and your sound began to mean
the same thing and the next thing you know there
were dictionaries and you and I could not only love each other,
but fight with each other too and we began to make
long contracts saying who would own what when.
It may be only yowling for all we know, all cawing back and forth
to say the same thing: someone is in charge and we'll make
sure we know who it is. Meanwhile the crows are calling
from tree to tree, rising up from the limbs on the gray day
and filling the sky with the other language of their wings,
how before we began to speak we could feel the world
inside our bodies and it moved us as we moved with it.
Perhaps this is our mother tongue, the language of our cells,

the diction of our hearts and lungs. There, don't say
anything for a while, don't even think in words,
think in whatever is beyond the thought of words,
the nameless world that you try so hard to forget
by naming everything. Take away the caws from the sky,
take away the rumble from the ice and while you're at it
take away the hiss of today's headlines, like air leaking
out of the world. See what's left after that and listen to it.

Back Then

I am not allowed in the hospital when I am five,
I am not allowed to see my grandfather dying,
those moments are reserved for adults
or someone who is at least sixteen,
as if those extra years prepare you
for seeing someone passing out of this life.
I am not allowed at the cemetery either,
not allowed to see the hole dug in the ground,
watch the coffin be lowered on a spring day,
the spring days when daffodils and forsythia
break yellow across all the green.
It's too much, they think, for young minds
to bear, not existing anymore, when there's
really nothing to worry about, because
young minds can't imagine not existing anymore.
Perhaps though with the first death we can see
it's going to end, if not for us, then for someone else
and someone else after that. Heaven isn't
out there calling. The mourners throw the first spadeful
of dirt on the coffin lid, hear the small rocks
and earth hit the surface, the sound reminds them
that it's not a dream, that this is really happening.
We are not allowed in hospitals, and not allowed
in cemeteries, we are only allowed in the safe places
of the world, where we can learn to become ourselves.
This is the story of any childhood, how we learn
first things first, how we skate and fall and skate and fall.
All around us the adult world is living its adult life,
smoking cigarettes, having opinions and electing Eisenhower,
building new roads and leaving the old world behind.
The earth hits the coffin, the daffodils bloom.
There is no sadness. It's the life we bring
to it that holds the sadness, like a monk
wandering with his begging bowl,
we hold the sorrow in our hands
and offer it to the world, thinking
it's all we have. Better to think of it

as a bird, something you've captured.
Toss it up into the sky, giving it an assist
as it takes wing into the day. Let it fly
over the graves, let it roost in the maple trees
where the branches are thick with buds,
let it lift in the warming air of spring.
Let sorrow drift over this day,
drift and roost again.

Opening a Savings Account, Crestmont Savings and Loan

This is the world that you'll invest in,
first with the passbook saving account
that has the dramatic weight of a passport,
something that passes through the hands
of the important people of the world.
Even the air inside the bank has a presence
an atmosphere of no fooling around, like the bookish air
inside the library and the sacred air inside the synagogue.
Outside the bank, the traffic moves over the old trolley tracks
that will soon be torn up and turned into something else:
weapons or cars or buildings. You're too young
to know that one thing becomes another
and that everything is changing around you all the time.
Now you think if you push the button on the pole at the cross walk,
you can actually make the light turn faster, if you press it continually
it will change right away, because you think you are in control
you think that the world begins with one place and moves
slowly out, as if your town is the Garden of Eden,
or at least a village at the beginning of the world.
The bank tellers, the teachers, the librarians
and the rabbi all had lives outside their uniforms
even if they couldn't speak of it themselves.
It's not the life you read about in the paper,
which the commuting fathers could tuck under their arms
on the way to the train, it's not in the advertisements
or in the headlines, it's not on the radio stations,
and wouldn't even be broadcast over the civil defense
emergency broadcast system. It's another life,
it's waiting to be asked questions, it's waiting to dance,
it's waiting to make love, it's waiting to weep and exhale
cigarette smoke, flick the ashes out the window,
where they catch the wind and drift. The other life
is drifting over the town, it's growing out of the maple trees,
it's in the forsythia, so bright and yellow
announcing itself all at once.

Fresh-Cut Grass

This is where my great career
as a second baseman will begin,
between the rhododendron that makes
a hiding place next to the brick wall

of our home and the sloping yard
rolling downhill to the slate sidewalk.
On the far end, the big silver maple
that once guarded the old house

of our ancient neighbor who died there
and, close by, the curb with the storm sewer
where all balls eventually find their way.
My glove is ready, the Stan Musial four-fingered

model that I've prepped over the winter the way
my big brother does, oiled with the ball in place
and a belt fastened around it, to make
the perfect pocket. I'm ready for the game.

I want to wear this glove, to break it in
so that the leather will be blackened and shiny
and I will catch everything, the short hop,
hard grounders, the line drives.

That I am skinny and left-handed may be
a drawback for my prospects of being
an infielder for the Yankees, but it's not stopping me now.
I throw the ball in the air I run under it,

calling off all of the imaginary teammates.
It's rising in the sky in this stadium,
this white planet of possibility
I'm searching for in the vast blue sky.

Unwritten History

I am wandering like everyone else
in the brief moment in history,
which some people see as cyclical
and others as linear,
but if you're an Aztec or Egyptian
or Mesopotamian, you're dead now
or what is left of you has been bred
and mixed with so many
other people that we are carrying on
the story without even knowing it.
It's in our cells that were once sloshing around
the now dry ocean beds of forgotten continents,
before anyone was naming anything.
This history goes back so far
it forgets itself and tells
the same few stories over
and over again.
I was born, the sun rose and fell,
I threw a ball in the air,
I caught it and ran, I imagined the world
and then made myself dizzy on a swing,
twisting and twisting the rope
and then looking at the tree branches
or my sneakers as the earth unwound itself.
I staggered off the seat and fell
on my back in the grass, the clouds were spinning,
the earth was heaving, the shrubs and rooftops,
in the altered state of my dizziness,
my highly evolved brain taken out
for a shakedown cruise in the whirling world.
Beyond the blue sky
the stars, turning themselves on and off,
spreading out beyond
the daily disasters and shadows, beyond the cold wind
and the first breath of thawed air. Sometimes
it's just a matter of getting started and sometimes
it's a matter of where you stop. Beginning and ending.

The middle always where it's supposed to be,
only I don't know how long its going to last because
God is no pilot coming on the intercom to welcome me aboard
and tell me how high I am or when I'll be landing
or to thank me as I look out the window
at the small finite world below and at the clouds
that the poets are drifting on, wandering across in the blue day.

Prayer for Beginning

You'll never know how it will end
and most days you don't even know
how it will begin. Will it be
a clean slate day, a morning
when you carry nothing
from the past into now,
or will your mind be loaded up
like a small U-Haul, filled
with the imagined words
of your father, last night's dream,
something you shouldn't
have said the night before
and a truck down-shifting
outside your window, so you put the key
into the soul's ignition and start driving
down the road where the sleeping houses
reveal themselves slowly in the dawn
and the birds are calling to the light.
Another day alive and singing.

Big World

It's a big world out there, big enough to encompass John Cage
and Popeye the Sailor all at once, big enough to encompass a monk
breathing the must of incense and a guy outside the bar exhaling
cigarette smoke and stamping his feet against the cold.
It's big enough to encompass miracle products that clean our houses
and the dirt that's entering our lives with every step.
It's a big enough world to encompass sleeping and waking.
A man tells himself to remember his dreams, but wakes
to find only ashes and feels the brush of a wing against his cheek.
The world is everyone dreaming stories all at once
and telling them in different ways. The world is the simplest
of things, opening a paper to see if your team won. And why not?
Won't everything fade and at least for the moment there is one
bit of order, there were nine innings, there were 27 outs
and something happened. It had to happen because we've
made a framework for it. It's the framework that gives the meaning.
All around us people have built churches and schools,
made the framework we can sit inside and made the rules
for the framework too, set the timer and told us when to get to work.
The world is a big enough place to encompass every idea
and every religion and every dream, but we've managed
to back them all into the same room where they begin
to knock against each other and growl. The world is big enough
to encompass every idea and every disease and the world
is big enough to encompass its own random self too.
John Cage is making a score for us to recognize
the randomness and Gertrude Stein is humming along,
and humming along and humming along and humming along,
but even they want to have their coffee at a specific time
in the morning, even they want some order to know
the world is alright. Some days all you can do is breathe.
All you can do is tie your shoes and put one foot in front of the other.
It's enough to make you weep, these simple steps.

Morning Prayer

In the early morning when I am
awake, but only to myself,
I put away the dishes, find
the right spots for the pot lids
to nestle, and assign the spatulas
and spoons to the right drawers.
It is a moment when, whatever
disarray awaits, things are in order:
forks are forks and bowls are bowls.
I reach for the first clean plates
and I remember a meditation: to wash
each dish as if God were coming
to dinner and can hold this thought
for a moment as I lift the porcelain cup
out of the drainer as if it's a vessel
full of the original light that is sweeping
the tips of the trees across the cove.
I remember this every morning,
an amnesiac at the sink, the coffee
brewing itself again.

Aperture

To let the light in
is to let the world in,
to have it draw itself

on our eyes everyday
so that we might see what's there:
the trees that rise and fall,

the horizon that separates
one thing from another,
a whole heaving planet

filled with those things
we have made of ourselves
and our shadows

as if it's possible to separate
the one from the other
in this bath of light

that is being absorbed
and reflected
by our hearts.

Classroom

Over the chalkboard the perfect alphabet
was written in upper and lower case letters,

so round and so straight, followed by 0 to 9,
the symbol systems for civilization

posted above our young heads.
All the letters that were waiting to speak to us

and us to them, and then just the ten numbers,
which puzzled me, since there were so many.

Why only those, I asked my brother,
older and smarter, because that's

all you need to make the rest he said,
a thought so big that it was larger

than a classroom or a playground,
that you can make more

from what you have, you can take
a one and as many zeroes as you'd like

and begin to make something really big,
become a millionaire or show

how many miles we are from the sun,
making everything out of that simple zero,

the circle with nothing in it, or the circle
with everything in it, a silent messenger, so quiet

all these years, whether we were fighting
Germans or Russians or Vietnamese or Iraqis

the circle above our heads as if we had a secret Buddhist message
in all our classrooms, the ones with the microbe-ridden carpets

or the ones with varnished oak floors,
the clock ticking and ticking

while above us the zero hovers, the reminder
of nothing and everything, the circle we can turn

into wheels of a bike and roll away
from here, from time,

and from the multiplication tables
that keep adding everything up.

Correct

You don't enter school knowing
how to cheat, but you

learn it by osmosis, how to get your
eyes over to your neighbor's desk,

the one that's better organized than
yours, catch the right answers

and write them on your own mimeographed
worksheet that you hope will be

marked with the big red C
meaning correct, because

you figure out quickly that correct is
all around you, in the line to the gym

in the line to the water fountain, in how
you smile or learn to raise your hand.

Cheating is like a chain letter or when you play
telephone. Someone else's eyes

are on your desk too, everyone
is looking for what's right and our

eyes are wandering. It's a wonder we learn
anything at all, all the while our skills increasing,

writing someone else's Latin translation
lightly in pencil over the nominative and accusative

of Caesar's battles or inking the hardness scale
of minerals on the sides of your fingers or

your sweating palm. We're not talking about
ethics here, we're talking about how we

survive, as if you're writing your own
fortune in your hand.

How Full Is This Life

When the snow falls on the tree for the first time
it's the sound of winter, one tick at a time
on the spruce needles and beech leaves,
like an old greeting.

When the phone rings it could be
good or bad news, but whatever you are expecting
is already in your heart with each ring,
like an emotional caller ID.

When I hear the poem for the first time
or I am really listening for the first time
then the room has a space in it, a space
big enough to hold an idea, a heart, or a life.

When the sounds all stop, or when the snow
is making its silence, I am listening to the world
just before it began, or just after it ended.
Sometimes they are the same thing.

When I am on the earth, there is something
under the ground, the trickle of water
through the fissures in the granite,
tiny cracks that rivers can pass through.

December Night

On the bus on the way home from Boston to Bangor
there's a movie playing, a comedy about a zookeeper
the animals decide to speak to because he's a nice guy
and is trying to marry the woman of his dreams
who winds up not being the woman of his dreams.
That one, of course, is beautiful and works right beside him.

He just needs to realize this. I don't really watch the movie,
but can take in enough of it to get this, can even look it up
on the internet to find out who's in it, all the while
the bus is moving forward in the December night,
the night that starts at four in the afternoon
and we travelers hurtling forward along route 95,

the mother and son who were visiting another son
in intensive care in Portland, the young man
who talks on the cell phone and tells his father
to shut up when it seems he's being asked
about his plans or how he got into whatever trouble
he got into that's bringing him home.

The young woman across from me makes
a quick call to home to say she's completed
the semester and done well, but whoever
is listening on the other end is not impressed enough,
doesn't recognize her accomplishments, and I can hear it in her voice.
Meanwhile on the little screens, the animals have decided

to break their code of silence and talk to the zookeeper.
If they could talk I'm sure they would be plotting
to eat the nearest zookeeper, however kind he might be, or
praying together for something better or else they might just
talk to themselves and sit in the corners of the cages.
Back on the bus the movie has ended and the credits are rolling.

It's only 6:30, but it feels as if has been dark forever,
even with the full moon rising, it is still dark, the kind of night

we could wander in and see the shape of things we recognize,
only they are holding the silence of dark, when you can only
begin to describe things. It's the kind of night our ancestors
would have watched the sparks from their fires rising heavenward

and in the forest the animals would have been moving in the night
or roosting in the trees, listening to the earth spinning as it turns
into late night and then the dawn. It's turning and turning again,
the cages are opening and everyone is coming out, taking
their rightful place among the living.

Scattered

in memoriam Ingrid Menken

Whether we spend our time
fearing death or not, listening
for its footsteps or plugging

our ears, we all end up
where we began, just dust
combined with the weight

of what we carried around in the world.
We reach into the plastic bag
and feel the ash and bone

of your body. We spread these
in small pinches at first,
watching the tide come up to the shore.

It pulls you back as it recedes,
as if you've gone for another
paddle in your kayak.

We place you in the water
of the bog along the path
and the milky white ash is like

the deep reflection of a cloud
in the still water.
Then the breeze picks up

and we toss what remains in the air.
We can hear the heavier
fragments of bone tick on the ledge,

like the way the gulls drop
mussel shells to crack them open,
but the rest of you rises

in the wind off the water,
an undulating column,
holding its shape, we can see it,

holding together as one
until it reaches the spruce on the shore.
It's October, but it looks

like pollen in spring air
or a galaxy expanding
into whatever is next.

Words for It

Even though we have so many words
we continue to make up new ones like *internet*
and *vitamin* and phrases like *weapons*
of mass destruction and in that way we
can continue to build a world of sound.
The sentences leave our mouths and
move the way all sound waves do,
never ending but getting quieter and quieter as they
vibrate, so that the long-lost first words
like the proto-Indo-European for *creation* or *seed*
are still traveling in the air.
Listen, can you feel the faint vibrations
on your eardrum, can you feel the ancient syllables
spiral into the ear canal.
Words are whispering to us
and we hear only the ones
we are ready for.
What if we opened the portals a little wider,
then we would be able to hear everything.
What if we could shout *forgiveness* and *pity*,
so that they could travel into everyone's ears.
How they could enter the mind at night or
how we could shout *empathy* and *love*…
Well, you get the idea. Only everyone is shouting
too much already, the words are bumping
into one another, sound waves on a roiled
ocean of syllables. What if we were all
quiet for a moment until things settled down,
the waters were flat calm, the storm had passed,
and it was one of those beautiful blue mornings
where it feels as if the world is born again,
which it is. You say *now* and the word leaves your lips
and begins its journey, buffeted
by the air from birds' wings, the sun's heat,
the thermal currents rising off the water and the mountains,
circling until it finds your ear again and you begin to listen.

Prayer for Mistakes

The last mistake you made
is not the end of the world,
the end of the world will be
much bigger than that,
much larger than you
and the last nightmares you had,
much bigger than your impossible to-do list
or any aches and pains that might be
sending signals to your brain.
So your brain can take a break
worrying about the end of things
and get started on now,
which is always the time
to get started on now,
always the beginning that is
whispering to you
with love and pity,
whispering for you
to almost hear.

Prayer for Real

One morning right after the rain
we were talking with the Gods
about whether we had imagined
them or they had imagined us.
The ground was soaked so we all knew
something was for real, but no one
was so sure about where meaning comes from,
which could be anywhere at any moment,
because meaning is a wild animal that surprises you
stepping out into the road at dusk,
meaning is a seed hidden in the ground,
meaning is a hungry world to feed,
so many hungers in this world,
real and imagined.

Prayer to Wake Up

This morning I wake and it's
cold in my room in the cool
stony shade of the building, but
if I walked outside I'd
find the sun working its way
through the alleys, sending long
shadows on the broken stones
and I would be in a different
world although it's really all
the same world, the movement
from dark to light to cold
to heat where everyone goes about
their work, the roosters crowing,
the dogs on the roof barking,
the old woman sweeping the sidewalk
with a broom, at first I was going
to say a tired broom, but its not
tired, it's just shaped by hand,
it's worked for many years
keeping things clean, making it possible
to start anew every morning.

Prayer for Survival

Is the world still here? Should
I look at the headlines first to
make sure, or is it enough to listen
to a delivery truck drive by over
worn out roads or hear the crows
moving through the pale air to roost
on bare branches or is it enough
to wake up and be breathing
and know that daylight exists again
that we are still turning
on our wobbly axis, turning
toward spring, toward blossom
then away from blossom,
white petals softly touching earth.

Prayer for Time

I write today's date and the year, 2011,
imagine 2020 and remember 1961,
which you can turn upside down
and still get the same number,
when will that happen again,
not for thousands of years,
and if we were writing back then,
the year 1111 would have been the best of all,
you could write that one in your sleep
unless people might also think you
were counting to four, one more line diagonally
and you're up to five, like a prisoner in a cell
keeping track of the days of incarceration.
We keep track of the days of freedom,
but not with that intensity, not carving
right into the wall like a tattoo of the hours,
all around us the seconds descending
like the latest weather.

Prayer for Knowledge

What I don't know could fill a book
fill all its hand-bound pages
with equations and history
and why worry about what
I don't know how about worrying about
the books I've written already, like the book
of the heart, with the pages that are inscribed
and erased every day and next to it
the book of the soul, written in a language
I used to speak, how to become
fluent in the syntax of love,
the vocabulary of each moment.

Prayer in the Dark

In the middle of the night
at the renovated armory turned

into a hotel in Portland I hear
coyotes yipping on the street

while you hear the cry of gulls
circling overhead, until rising

out of our dreams we realize
it's not the wild world outside

but the couple making love
in the room next to us and we

have heard this through the wall,
but it is just as natural, this wildness

that calls out in their throats
this cry from within yearning

to get out, this ancient impulse
in the forest of the night, how

we have all emanated from these same
yips and cries and begun our journey.

The Passage

My friend lies in the nursing home bed,
eyes closed, her breathing shallow and labored.

She is ninety-three and just a few months before
was tending geraniums and putting black

sunflower seeds in her bird feeder,
but now she is ready to let go.

She barely whispers to me, "This is hard work,"
while across the darkened room, Dora moves

in and out of farm houses she lived in
and has conversations with the people she knew.

Then she suddenly sits upright and shouts at me
"Do you think about us? Do you pray for us?"

not knowing who I am, but lucid and with an urgent
need to know my answer. What do you say when

someone looks you in the eyes? The room holds
only three of us, past, past, and present,

so there is only one person to respond, and I say
"Yes, yes" the first time trying out the answer

the second time believing it. Somewhere near my heart
I should light the candles, and whisper all the names.

If Poetry is a Prayer for Looking Deeply

Then each day is special, not because Macy's
is having a sale on coffee pots, flatware,
towels, cookware, convection ovens, and as many bras
as you'd ever need, but because in the autumnal air,
the late air of November 18th, the only red
is in the winter berries' fragile light
reflecting into the world,
which today is drying out after a week of rain
and it feels like the old world
is starting over again, which it is, crows flying
over a newly revealed planet as it spins
into the light. The eiders plummet
into the blue, diving to a depth
I'll never know, small bird lungs
full of air. It's the deep descent
into the everyday that we are after,
the moment that will make the tap water holy,
the first breath a blessing. This is how the holy ones
go through life, thanking God for every ritual of the body
every mouthful of food, every movement of the bowels.
For what can't be holy, what can't we transform
from profanity past loneliness and terror
into holiness? Today the overflowing ponds look
toward heaven and the sky answers back
with a deep blue *amen*.

The Naturalist

The yellow returns to the finches over the winter,
bit by bit, so in February when everything is dull
they are too, then gradually, right before my eyes
everyday at the feeder, they add more yellow to their feathers,
as if they are taking the growing light of the sun
into their wings and breast, which they are.
It's the before-our-eyes business that I'm interested in,
how it's all happening in front of us, or sometimes
in our rear view mirror or in our peripheral vision.
The birds take flight from the feeder,
20 or 30, and rise like a blanket of energy into the birch or the air
and are gone. Keeping track of them is a part of my work.
I'd like to tell you that I keep a bird journal. I'd like to be a writer
who sits in the same place everyday and watches the changes
of the world, the gradual flow of one color to the next,
the leaf dropping so that I can hear it as it hits the ground
and rocks slightly in the long grass.
I'd like to tell you that I've been looking all the time,
that my powers of observation are as keen
as a 19th century naturalist or a cinematographer for a PBS special
only we're not in the steamy jungle or in a Land Rover
on the savannah or the pressurized deepness
of the ocean, we're in my backyard where these
transformations happen in real time, the daffodils
breaking ground and piercing last year's fallen leaves
with the power of its upward thrust,
the maple seeds burrowing in the ground as my house spins
at 70,000 miles per hour around the sun, which is making
the world yellow and green, and even with all that velocity,
my hair isn't moving at all and my pants aren't billowing out.
I'm standing in the still point then,
waiting for the heat from the equator to turn itself into wind
that will shake the branches that will send my birds away
from the feeder, that will scatter the sunflower seeds to the ground,
where they will begin to remember the journey earthward
that they never knew, the same way the finch looks at its wings
turning yellow and greets this news as a surprise, as if it has never

happened before. That's the way to wake to the world, changing in every moment, breathing the light of the sun, remembering what you don't know and learning what's always been inside you.

Wild God

There was a time when God ran wild through the Garden,
when the earth was new and the animals hadn't been named yet.
God ran wild like the wind through the trees. The crows
were calling out to all the other creatures in their dark voices,

Wild God on the way, watch out, for in the right frame of mind,
God could make the land tremble, make the mountains low
and the valleys rise up. Meanwhile the grass kept growing,
the soft grass of the pastures growing long enough

to wave in the light. God liked to stop being wild
for a while just lying back and seeing the future
in the clouds and marveling at this work
of the holy hands. Even wild ones settle down

and rest every now and then and begin to imagine
making a place where someone will
fear no evil, imagine goodness and mercy unleashed on the world.
But then it's time to get up and run again, God being

young and all too. Run wild in a thunderous world,
one big footstep at a time. There are days to make animals
and there are days to talk with the angels. Days to wander
among your children and in each one recognize a certain

resemblance. Days to go home and weep and think
how hard it is, not to create, but to handle
the extended maintenance of the whole enterprise,
not the beginning and the end, which will probably be simple,

but the middle. The long middle when the plan is not so clear,
the past making the present, the present the future,
like it's some conveyor belt of the cosmos.
God isn't bone tired yet, but getting a little tuckered out

with trying to get it right, just right, with every line in place,
with every word the right one, just the way any artist
would want to make it. One wild world at a time,
one wild god running the show.

Prayer for Today

Today this morning December 22
the day after we re-lit the hot water heater
when the pilot light blew out, two days
after the lunar eclipse at the winter solstice
when the bronze light shadowed the constellations
whose names I do not know, distant, distant light
out of which we make patterns to tell our stories,
or patterns may be something that are always there
and I only need my eyes to guide me,
my eyes and my heart, which is always
open for business, on call 24/7 pumping the news
out into the world, like headlines
running through a web press: Extra Extra
Read All About It:
Alive Again Today.

The Holy One

after a painted wooden figure by an anonymous maker

We can find holiness anywhere, even if a while ago
this saint was hanging from a rafter in a garage in Taxco, Mexico
and flew through Chicago to Boston to Bangor and passed

through security screening in two countries and was wrapped
in a newspaper describing the latest disaster,
whether it was child abuse or pollution or terror or illiteracy or

too much of everything in an overstuffed world, whether the person
who carved or painted the soft wood even intended holiness with it,
it arrives before us. His arms gesture out in a sermon of color and air,

one arm raised to speak to the slate gray water and illuminated
white gulls that lift themselves in flight, a flight that is also holy
and unlikely, as if they rose up out of the air when our wooden saint

lifted his arms. That used to be a small miracle of the dump,
when the gulls picked at the open garbage. Stand still, raise
both arms slowly, like two giant wings, and the gulls

rise in unison, floating on nothing, the same way the saint delivers
a sermon, one airy word at a time, one ethereal syllable
that takes flight and reaches into the ears of the penitent and the lost,

reaches into the ears and burrows into the hearts like a divine parasite
that eats from the inside out. You know the way people used to say
what's eating you, which implies something under your skin

or working its way in. The saint preaches to all of us who have
something devouring our own souls, because that's when
we are ready to listen. He raises his enormous hands,

he opens his gigantic eyes, their lashes like the wings of butterflies
or tiny angels, and speaks slowly, whispering and eventually
not even saying words, just letting air pass through his lips,

because breath and spirit were once the same word,
and his breath travels out in the world
like the air when you open the windows after winter,

like the air the milkweed drifts on in the fall, the air full
of seeds and promise. These are the moments the saint
brings us when we are ready, whether we are holy or not,

crawling on paving stones or marching along the highway
with our candles lit, their tenuous light flickering
in the breezes of darkness. This is the darkness that we

ought not curse, but just realize that we are swimming in it,
a night swim, afloat on the unseeable, the unknowable.
This is where we are drifting today, listening for your voice. *Amen.*

Open Window

In the perfect cartoon world
the pie is placed to cool at the window,

the fragrance of apple and cinnamon
rising in the air, air that is all excited

molecules that spend their days
moving around the world, carbon

and oxygen molecules and if I've
got this right, we're all

breathing the same oxygen
and in every twentieth breath

I'm inhaling the air that Columbus
took into his lungs. But it's not just my cilia

and his cilia that have tickled the same
atoms, but also Moses, and Pablo Neruda,

and my grandmother and you as well.
In that way we are all one,

living, dying, re-forming, the apple
pie we steal from the window becoming us,

becoming earth, becoming tree
becoming fruit, becoming seed.

Look at the beautiful white blossoms
in the spring rain, traveling on the sweet air.

Worries

We're always worrying about things, usually worried
about things that won't happen, the way last week
someone told me that he was always worried
he'd make some mistake and end up a bum on the Bowery.
He'd finally realized that now that he was sixty
and lived in Vermont, that probably wouldn't happen.
It's no matter, we can still worry about it, we can fill
rooms, houses, small villages with our worries
and still we would need more room for them.
I don't think animals worry, although there is the way
that dogs furrow their brows when they're trying to figure out
if you are coming or going. Or else we like to think they're worried
because it makes us feel better that we do.
Maybe it's just me. Maybe you're not worried about anything,
you're Mr. Happy-Go-Lucky, you're Ms. Not-A-Care-in-the-World,
Maybe you've just learned how to exhale and let everything off your
chest or off your back or wherever these worries swarm and cluster.
Maybe you enjoy watching them fly off like a migration
of monarch butterflies, on determined little wings.
That helps you get a little distance, when you can see your worries
flutter, have elaborate courting rituals, travel by instinct,
and know how to survive. You don't have to worry
about your worries! They are able to take care of themselves.
They are able to manage on their own. Once you've let them go,
they float in whichever direction the wind blows,
they float in the wind and mix with desires, dreams, and memories.
It's like a reunion without you. You're free of them
and it looks like they don't need you anymore either.
But seeing them float outside you, don't you miss them?
They are your children who have gone from home.
Don't you want to hold them one more time,
caress their foreheads, memorize the shape of their faces,
look into their dark eyes, which are filling
with tears and looking back at you?

Breath

All morning I have been breathing, ever since
I awoke, in and out, and before that, all night
even through my dreams and before that when
I was driving home in the dark. One breath in

and one breath out, hundreds an hour,
thousands a day, how quickly our breaths
must equal the population of a small city,
every breath an unconscious affirmation of life—

for what else keeps us alive except this simple
gesture bringing air into our lungs and the news
from outside into our bodies. We breathe life in
and exhale our existence out into the world,

whether it's a deep hopeful breath or
a shallow one of fear, it enters and exits
our lives and joins us to everything. There are
the times when you wonder what if you stopped

breathing, what if you didn't think about it,
but our bodies are smart beyond us and won't
let us die just because we aren't thinking about it,
we can override our own minds and keep going,

up until the last breath, when you send
yourself out into the day for the last time,
where the warm air of your lungs drifts
like a small cloud until the molecules separate and go

their own ways, like it's after graduation and old
friends are saying farewell, leaving to make their fortunes.
The last of you, your breath, riding on the air
and someone breathes you in, takes you into

their lives for a moment, just as you have
inhaled someone else's last moment.

We are passing each other around, molecule
by molecule. I've just taken you inside me now

and sent you off into winter day, for this is a planet
of all used parts, and there is nothing that is not made
of something else, formed and re-formed. Nothing
is lost, it's circling around us, and even if we vanish

like a wisp of smoke, somewhere we are breathed in again,
just as the world is breathing in and out, one enormous
pulse of water and light and stone, a breath within
another breath and we breathe for each other,

and the plants breathe for us, as if it's CPR all the time,
sending air around the branches of our lungs, out
to the very end of the alveoli, as if the Tree of Life
is inside us, our own Garden of Eden.

Leaving the Country

Because everything will fade,
I begin writing on the bus

on the way to the airport,
wanting to save the details

of the green world, of the hillsides
stitched together with stone walls,

the sheer drop of the cliffs to the swirling water
and the ancient stone oratory, on which divine light

falls everyday, but also to remember
the woman in Dingle telling us her husband used

to fish until his boat 'went against him' and the dark
beauty of the pints of stout, not to remember that

I have traveled here, but because there are some places
you know that you will never see again

and suddenly just before it is too late realize
how sweet it is to be alive,

because each day is in its way a small death
and there is no turning back.

What would you remember?
Would the fish and chips, steam rising

from it in the colder evening,
make you sing or weep?

How about the cry of the man
hawking newspapers at dusk,

or the fishmongers deftly wrapping
today's catch for you to take home?

Within We Are All Full of Light

Imagine the wonderment
of the people who built

the first *camera obscura*
and discovered that a stream of light

can tell us so much,
how one tiny hole in the wall

can let in the wavelengths
that draw a perfect picture.

It's upside down, which shakes us up,
but shows us that something

is watching us too, inscribing each detail,
steeple and leaf, hill and cloud,

making every color possible
and this morning when I go outside

and stare into the spring light being
absorbed and bouncing off

the gray stone walk and new dandelions,
I become my own darkened room

letting the day in to write its history
on the back wall of my mind. Light within,

light without, I close my eyes
to see what I have loved.

Forgiveness

"Something will tell you, 'This is it! Eureka!' If you still feel lonely in your heart, or bitterness, you'll know that you're not there." Anthony, in Jonathan Kozol's book *Amazing Grace*, describing heaven.

If you feel bitterness leave your heart,
it will float lightly in the sky like milkweed in a blue wind.

If it floats in the blue wind, other people will see it float by
and think that it is a thing of great ethereal beauty.

If it's a thing of ethereal beauty, it will float in the air
for a long time before it falls to earth.

If it falls to earth, it will bury itself in last year's decay
and return as a green shoot in spring.

If it returns as a green shoot in spring, it will grow into something
beautiful, as if it is a tree in the kingdom of heaven.

If it is a tree in the kingdom of heaven,
all the birds of the field will come to roost in it.

If all the birds of the field come to roost in it,
then they will begin to sing.

If the birds begin to sing all at once, they will fill the dome
of heaven with their song and it will echo off the canyon walls below.

If it echoes off the canyon walls below, then we
will hear it and it will enter our hearts.

If it enters our hearts it will move through our bodies,
like a leaf floating on a stream.

If it floats like a leaf on a stream, it will be like an empty vessel
waiting to be filled with what we choose.

Heaven

Someone is always promising something in heaven,
and someone else is always revising
the regulations for entry. This is why

I've never started my own religion—
it would be too much to try to think
of who's in and who's out,

and too much to make up codes,
as if I am my own IRS of the Spirit
and I would have to create a priestly class of CPAs

just to interpret the regulations governing
what gets us in and to whom we bend our knees or not.
Up in the clouds, the sun is breaking through.

It's a day after a storm, which seems like a day after a battle,
when bewildered soldiers emerge from trenches
to begin to mourn the dead. In heaven,

there are too many dead to count.
I'm not a mathematician, but I know there
are more on the way, an exponential exodus,

with some looking for virgins, some for their families,
some for the perfect place to hunt.
But heaven is more like TV before cable and satellite,

and we have only rabbit ears to bring us a ghost of a picture.
Looking through that static and snow,
we can help ourselves by imagining what was there,

a picture made from radio waves
transformed into images, and those divine waves wash over us,
and lift us like the salt water at the shore,

in a buoyant caress. By then we are adrift
and not remembering our name or the names
of everyone we knew. We are only remembering

the patterns of sunlight and shadow, halos of light
against the sky. We are only remembering
the wind in the trees and the rain of imperfect love.

Extinction

All the Romans are dead and so is their language,
except that the ancestors of their words have found
their way into my pen and your pen
and onto the tongues of the Spanish, French,
and Portuguese. But the Romans are gone now, no longer
at the end of the sentence verbs placing, no longer
using prepositions like small mass transit systems
burrowing underneath your sentences. Latin is gone-by,
and the turntable was headed down that same road
only to be resurrected from 8-track oblivion, making a comeback
from garages and yard sales. Now it is transformed
to scratch at sound, the arm deciphering the vinyl imprint
following each echo and wave back to the first word.
My friend Bobby listened to the song *The Lion Sleeps Tonight*
so many times, eventually the grooves were worn smooth
and the record and the label circled around and around
at 45 revolutions per minute, soundlessly,
no more groove for the needle to listen to in this jungle
where the lion sleeps, the mighty jungle we walk into
when we are trying to find the first word to speak,
to name the first thing and find the words
that we have in common. That jungle must be on the edge
of the Garden of Eden, where the sound came from
before the Romans were here, before the Greeks were here,
before the past was perfect and everyone became tense.
Back then it was all one spinning around like the turntable
the slow circling or fast circling at 33 ⅓ or 45 or 78
each revolution changing the sound as if we could
speed things up or slow them down and make sense of them.
Spin the turntable backward and it's a different language—
it's rolling over what you've already heard only now
you are in the dyslexic heaven of your own mind—
you know, where god and dog run around together,
chasing each other, barking at the wind, rolling
on their backs in the grass and naming all the things
that we have created, one after one,
naming the sounds and hoping for the best.

How Could I Have Forgotten This?

The touch of the air, that is, right after winter has passed,
remembering that everything is alive, that the fruit
in the supermarket, even the pears in cans, all came
from someplace where there was earth and water and sun
and that is, after all, all there is: earth, water, and sun to make
all this, to send the water up the trunks for the trees to make
the sweet sap that brings it to life. It all comes back.
It is always about the seed in the ground.
The seed in the ground never forgets, never forgets the way
up and out and the seed ensures the fruit that ensures the seed
that ensures the fruit. It's a different timeline than getting
from here to there. It's the timeline with no beginning
and no end, an entire history in a small vessel,
just the way we are entire histories in sperm and egg,
so much memory and so little time. The seeds work their way
back into the ground or are eaten or carried away or float
over the landscape like milkweed and if we could stand
on a hillside in the sunlight we would see the air full of seeds,
drifting but not drifting aimlessly, drifting with purpose,
the purpose of survival and this is the way to get there.
There are many ways to survive, many ways to go on living.
Some days it's only floating in the wind, high in the wind,
the wind that can even make the trash look beautiful,
the white plastic bags from the convenience store
inflated from underneath, tumbling over and over
as traffic rushes by, until it gets caught up in the trees
and waves like a prayer flag an unknowing blessing
over all of us, the receipt backlit by the sun like an x-ray
of the small bills that we've paid.

Morning Headline

We reach from the darkness into the day,
find what we thought we knew carried away
facing just the headlines of what has already passed,

the price of milk, of bread, of gas
and not only that, but of all the disasters
that have gone before our eyes.

The news perhaps is best to burn,
watch the flame's ashes flutter and turn
over and over in the landscape of what we know.

The fields are flooded with an orange glow
as if the light will flow over the earth
and into our own hearts

as if we are ready to make a new start
by harnessing the elements to one another,
earth to air and fathers to brothers

a family of spirit singing for only us to hear it,
not the meaning but the sound,
not the chaos but the roundness

of all that is whole. And even if we don't
recognize the essence within every surprise
even if we don't care for the moment, it's here.

Exhale

I haven't smoked cigarettes for years
but I can still remember
the long exhale that came
after the long inhale
as if I had taken something big,
like grief, into my body
and had it swim in my lungs,
how with a cigarette you are breathing
and dying at the same time,
which is what gives us
that subtle pleasure when we ignite it
from the glowing lighter coil in the car
and the first breath is in our bodies,
the smoke trailing out the open window.
Besides the warning on the pack
that tells us that smoking can kill us,
there should be a second note telling us that
smoking can cause remorse, when we exhale
all that we are not, when we savor the moment
with the cup of coffee, the moment that reminds us
that we are living and dying at the same time
and it is that moment when mortality
snaps us awake and we want to
run from the truth and embrace it.
In that way cigarettes are a religious ritual:
behold this light, behold
this plant of the earth, join them together
and realize that it will all become ash.
One day we are sitting around a table
and then we are an empty chair.
Let me smell your hair,
let me inhale you like all that is transient:
the wispy spirit of our lives that rises
to heaven and makes clouds not out of water
but of grief and joy with a few heavy
metals and carcinogens thrown in,
this sacrament that is as solid as air,

that is drifting in the wind
and looking for nothing.

Question Prayer

Where do prayers begin?
I think in the same place that memories
are born: the headwaters of the soul
where from nowhere the rivers start
with a trickle and drip in silence
how the waters gather up, all those streams
of doubt and courage soon rushing over
everything to change rocks, to move
earth and stone, to etch something
it will eventually make flat, the record
of the journey erasing itself.

Prayer for Joy

What was it we wanted
to say anyhow, like today
when there were all the letters
in my alphabet soup and suddenly
the 'j' rises to the surface.
The 'j', a letter that might be
great for scrabble, but not really
used for much else, unless
we need to jump for joy,
and then all of a sudden
it's there and ready to
help us soar and to open up
our hearts at the same time,
this simple line with a curved bottom,
an upside down cane that helps
us walk in a new way into this
forest of language, where all the letters
are beginning to speak,
finding each other in just
the right combination
to be understood.

Holding the Light

for Kait Rhoads

Gather up whatever is
glittering in the gutter,
whatever has tumbled
in the waves or fallen
in flames out of the sky,

for it's not only our
hearts that are broken,
but the heart
of the world as well.
Stitch it back together.

Make a place where
the day speaks to the night
and the earth speaks to the sky.
Whether we created God
or God created us

it all comes down to this:
In our imperfect world
we are meant to repair
and stitch together
what beauty there is, stitch it

with compassion and wire.
See how everything
we have made gathers
the light inside itself
and overflows? A blessing.

Only Now

Only now
do you realize
how quickly
everything
passes
how we
are here for
a blink of God's eye
how the light passes
by us and through us
how the world
began with a breath
and a cry
earth and sky.

Eternity

The door is always open.
It swings gently back and forth

in the breeze. Birds fly effortlessly
in and out through open windows.

None break through the panes of glass.
Blue clouds float on the white air.

The same letters come everyday.
It's not all good news, although

all of your poems have been accepted.
Some of it is news from long ago

some are the headlines of what
hasn't happened yet. You read

each letter as if every word is new
and just what you needed to hear.

It begins to rain—a light shower—
just enough water to smell the earth

just enough water to settle
all the dust.

Acknowledgments

Thanks is due the editors of publications where some poems in this collection have appeared.

Rocky Coast—Narramissic Notebook

Prayer in the Dark—Words and Images

Heaven—Words and Images

Within We Are Full of Light—Signs of Life

Open Window—Maine Magazine

Forgiveness—A Ritual to Read Together Poems in Conversation with William Stafford

If Poetry is a Prayer for Looking Deeply, Prayer for Beginning, Prayer to Wake Up, Prayer for Today, Prayer for Real, Question Prayer, Winter Morning Prayer, and *Prayer for Mistakes* were published as <u>A Deep Blue Amen</u>, a limited edition book (Amanda Degener/Cave Paper, 2013)

Thanks to the Haystack Mountain School of Crafts and the Vermont Studio Center for providing the time and space for me to work on some of these poems, and thanks as always to Susan, Isaac, and Sam for their wisdom, humor and encouragement.

Stuart Kestenbaum grew up in Maplewood, NJ and received a BA degree from Hamilton College. He has lived in Maine for many years, and since 1988 has been the director of the Haystack Mountain School of Crafts in Deer Isle. He is the author of three previous collections of poems, most recently *Prayers and Run-on Sentences* (Deerbrook Editions), and a collection of brief essays, *The View From Here* (Brynmorgen Press).